MONIQUE STUBBS-HALL

Love Ain't Pain Free

A Thought Provoking Poetic Collection of Blues, Love
and Motivation

TRAFFORD

Note for Librarians: a cataloguing record for this book that includes Dewey Decimal
Classification and US Library of Congress numbers is available from the Library and Archives of
Canada. The complete cataloguing record can be obtained from their online database at:
www.collectionscanada.ca/amicus/index-e.html
ISBN 1-4120-8796-1
Printed in Victoria, BC, Canada

*Printed on paper with minimum 30% recycled fibre. Trafford's print shop runs on "green energy" from solar, wind
and other environmentally-friendly power sources.*

TRAFFORD

Offices in Canada, USA, Ireland and UK
This book was published *on-demand* in cooperation with Trafford Publishing. On-demand
publishing is a unique process and service of making a book available for retail sale to the
public taking advantage of on-demand manufacturing and Internet marketing. On-demand
publishing includes promotions, retail sales, manufacturing, order fulfilment, accounting and
collecting royalties on behalf of the author.

Book sales for North America and international:
Trafford Publishing, 6E–2333 Government St.,
Victoria, BC V8T 4P4 CANADA
phone 250 383 6864 (toll-free 1 888 232 4444)
fax 250 383 6804; email to orders@trafford.com
Book sales in Europe:
Trafford Publishing (UK) Ltd., Enterprise House, Wistaston Road Business Centre,
Wistaston Road, Crewe, Cheshire CW2 7RP UNITED KINGDOM
phone 01270 251 396 (local rate 0845 230 9601)
facsimile 01270 254 983; orders.uk@trafford.com
Order online at:
trafford.com/06-0552

10 9 8 7 6 5 4 3 2

Love Ain't Pain Free

Preface

Ever felt like you were living a fairy tale life…riding off into the sunset with the one you love…heading for a life of eternal bliss and….

…OOPS!

You fell off the horse and woke up to the reality that your fairy tale Castle walls had crumbled around you. You were surrounded with piles of rubble…

…WHY OH WHY!

Had no one prepared you for the reality that "love ain't pain free"?

… THERE IS HOPE!

This collection of poetry is dedicated to you. Despite the pain, bumps, bruises, trials and errors you can pick up the pieces, build a new and improved Castle, find love again and ride off into the sunset, FOR REAL!

A Special Note From The Author

"My healing has come through journaling. It's amazing the empowerment that comes from thoughts of the heart flowing through ink onto the pad. I know that you may have many moments of pain as well as pleasure that utilizing this exercise will benefit you as well. So please take advantage of the journal pages that accompany each piece within my three collections.

After reading each selection, try immediately recording the feelings or experiences that come to mind from past or current situations within your personal life's journey. My desire is that you find inner peace and serenity and the ability to move forward as I have. Most importantly, may you be moved to not allow anyone or anything stop you from reflecting the beautiful qualities that you were created with, the qualities that make you, like a fingerprint, unique".

Enjoy Your Journey,

Monique

Funny…this thing called love

Intriguing it is

Intense it can become

Beautiful it can be made

Inspiring at times

Perfect when it's right

…but

Somehow they forgot to tell me

That

Love ain't pain free!

What's Inside?

* Feeling the Rhythm
* Traveling the Serengeti
* One Fall Day
* Wish I Could Have Been Your Sunshine
* Sumthin' 'Bout You
* The Pleasure's All Mine
* Passion
* Keeps Comin' Back To You
* Must Be Everlasting
* Soulwife

"Mo" tivation
   * From Birth to Death
   * Her Eyes Reveal It All
   * I Shall Be Victorious!
   * Never Abandon Hope
   * The Inner Me
   * Calm The Sea
   * Expansion
   * Black Man Show Me Your Strength
   * Falling Down
   * I Define Me
   * I Will Not Settle
   * "The Flow"
   * Mommy
   * Daddy

Acknowledgements
About the Author

"Mo" Blues

YES WITH LOVE THERE IS PAIN!

(Falling off your horse and realizing that your castle has crumbled around you is sobering, indeed)

13

MEMORY PAGE

_____

_____

_____

_____

_____

_____

_____

_____

_____

_____

_____

_____

_____

_____

_____

_____

Mending Broken Pieces

Like fine crystal glistening in the sunlight
Shining and sparkling at every angle
Delicately placed in your possession
Representing purity and clarity
Yes, that was me!

Taken down from your showcase
Hidden amidst common glassware
No longer glistening, but losing luster
Dull, from misuse, muddied from unclean hands
No longer recognizable as a cherished piece

Disrespected, misrepresented, left alone
Cast aside as useless, beauty hidden
Picked up and thrown down, shattered!

Then you realized my value
Tried to mend the broken pieces
Polished me up as best you could
Realized how much you loved me
I'm back in your showcase
Flawed, but back!

MEMORY PAGE

Do You Know What You Do To Me?

Do you know what you do to me?
Can you see it in my eyes?
You bring out the sunshine in me,
You clear my cloudy skies.

Do you know what you do to me?
Can you feel it in my touch?
You warm my inner being,
Having you near me means so much.

Do you know what you do to me?
Can you see me flying high?
I'm striving for levels I've never reached before,
Just your voice inspires me to try.

Do you know what you do to me?
Can you sense it in my kiss?
Your passion and tenderness is all there,
Don't you know I hunger for your bliss.

Do you know what you do to me?
Are your dreams a lot like mine?
Imagining the pleasure of making love to you,
And then trying to erase the thoughts from my mind.

Do you know what you do to me?
I don't know if you even have a clue,
You just send my world spinning,
Can I just run away with you?

Do you know what hurts me most?
I'm not with you everyday,
I must share in your joys from afar,
I must love you from a distance,
I can't cuddle in your arms,
You can't find my tender spots,
You can't strip off all my layers,
And feast your eyes on what awaits you.

I wish I could satisfy your every desire,
But right now it is not meant to be,
But I wanted you to know,
Just what you do to me.

MEMORY PAGE

_____

_____

_____

_____

_____

_____

_____

_____

_____

_____

_____

_____

_____

_____

_____

_____

_____

Lost At Sea

Love at first sight
That's what you always said
Our first few years
We shared a warm bed
Our love was tight
Yeah, it was tight!

My friends say the signs were there
I just refused to accept
This love we had was unique
Their implications I would reject
Yeah , you kept late nights
I thought it was a Man's thing
Even though you'd blow up when I asked where you'd been
Even though you kept misplacing your wedding ring

I kept missing the signs.....what was wrong with me?

I wanted to believe in you
I wanted to take your word
But I started finding receipts and other evidence
And you wouldn't believe the things I heard
After years of trying to give you the benefit of the doubt
I realized YOU had chosen to drift out

Why did it take me so long to see?

Baby, if you wanted that other life so bad
You should have just let me know
It would have hurt me
But had you told me straight...I would have let you go
Why did you wait until we had started a family,
If you knew you wanted to drift away from me?

It's not fair what you've done
You didn't even think of us
I loved you and loved you s'more now we've lost the trust
You've gotten what you wanted I guess

Freedom....was that what you wanted?
From what?
You just look lost to me…..
Baby you're out there……lost at sea

You've floated away from me
So gradually
I failed to notice at first
Now you've drifted too far away from me
You are no longer in view....you are lost at sea

Goodbye baby

Hope you find watcha lookin' for

'cause it's cold

Lonely

dark …out there

to drift was your choice

the elements are not kind

sail safely baby

sail

safely

MEMORY PAGE

Midnight Blues

Baby, where are you tonight?
Why do you leave me like this?
You've got to know this ain't right
Your dinner is still on the table, your company I miss

Do you think I don't wonder,
Are you working undercover?
Under whose covers are you?
When you are out doin' what you do?

Yes it's midnight baby
The clocks struck 12
It's midnight baby
You're not home where we dwell
Yes it's midnight baby
This bed's gettin' cold
Yes it's midnight baby
This patterns gettin' old

Baby it's been too many nights like this
My heart used to ache for you baby
I used to long for your bliss
You've done me wrong, in my heart I know
You took me for granted 'cause you thought
I had no place to go

But don't be so sure, sweet baby
You've left me alone too many nights
Someone will warm this bed, baby
Only then will you realize
You had a good thing here baby

Right here under your eyes

I'm tired baby,
Tired of waitin' up all night
Tired of wondering baby, whether you would make it home
each night
Were you hurt or were you out hurting me?
Tired of figuring it out and yet you just couldn't see
My heart's turned cold to you, baby
Cold as this bed I'm lyin' in
What I'm tryin' to tell you baby
Is I'm leavin' you for him!

He's fillin' this void
He's treatin' me well
He's lovin' me baby
He's here where we dwell
He's warmin' my bed

It's midnight baby and where are you?

'nough said

'nough said

'nough said!

MEMORY PAGE

_____

_____

_____

_____

_____

_____

_____

_____

_____

_____

_____

_____

_____

_____

_____

_____

_____

_____

_____

Strings Attached

You saw me standing there
This perfect picture of innocence
You hesitated to approach
But something drew you close
You've been a part of my life ever since

Yes it's true I come with strings attached
I'm tangled up within a web
Just wish you could come in to release them one by one
Then baby lead me to your bed

What a pity you say
That someone as sweet as me
Could be mistreated and misunderstood
But don't you realize
Fate brought us eye to eye
If you could release me, I know you would

I'm so sorry I come with so many strings attached
All tangled up within a web
Just wish you could come in to release them one by one
Then baby lead me to your bed

You made my heart skip a beat
I know you don't really have a clue
How much you've come to mean to me
What qualities in you I see
There's so much more I'd like to have of you

…But I know you run from me….

'Cause I have so many strings attached
Just tangled up within this web

Just wish you could come in and release them one by one
Then Baby lead me to your bed
Detach me

I'm caged in

No escape

Caught up in his web of lies

I'm begging

Unravel me

And Baby when I'm free
I will show you my gratitude
Come closer

Release me

Then
Lead
Me
To
Your
Bed!

MEMORY PAGE

It's Simple

Why do you take things to the level you do?
You're always trying to fit the wrong shoe
You take a small thing I say and turn it into a mountain
You keep spewing out remarks like a dog gone fountain!
You're too deep, honey
You take it too far, baby
You pull it apart, sugar
When it's simple, my love is simple

Just wrap me in your arms
Just tell me you care
Just look me in the eyes baby
And tell me you're here
Just respect me, that's all
Running late? Just a call
Show me the love, it's simple
My love is simple

You make all these excuses
'Lots of verbal abuses
You mask all my feelings
Despite my constant pleadings
You say I've changed and you don't know who I am
But I'm the same as I've been, you're the one that's the sham
It's simple, my love is simple

How much more breaking down can I do?
See the weight now is on you
It's your love that's so deep
You're the one losing sleep
Since loving you is so complicated, let's make a deal
Then we can move on and this relationship will be real!

My love is simple

It's simple!

MEMORY PAGE

_____

_____

_____

_____

_____

_____

_____

_____

_____

_____

_____

_____

_____

_____

_____

_____

Just One Regret

Came to town the other day
Caught a glimpse of you from afar
Hadn't seen you in so many years
Sent a flashback of pictures in my mind
Don't you know you were my shining star!

Just knew we would have been together
But then you moved away without a trace
You never knew my heart was torn in two
If only we had spoken more
You would have known in my heart for you
I had saved a special space.

Wish I could make you understand
My life is not the way I planned
I have just one regret it's true
I cannot spend my life with you
Wish I could turn back the hands of time
Then move them forward, so you'd be mine
Yes one regret it's true
I wanted to spend forever with you

Had no idea you had come back here
Would have never dreamed I would ever see you again
Never knew how I would feel if I did
Now I know because it happened
So quickly that empty feeling came back
Like when you left before and I felt I had lost my best friend

Funny you never knew that all the times we laughed
together
That all the times we cried on each other's shoulder
That all the times we spent hanging together

I had fallen deep in love with you
My one regret is I never let you know
And then you vanished, I regret I let you go

So I just let you walk on by without a word
Wanted to reach and touch you the way I used to
But I saw you walking with her hand in hand
What would be the use I thought it's too late now

So I quickly turned around
Faced my head towards the ground
Yes tears came down my eyes
Yes I cried for you it's true

The pain was still there
I wish you were mine
I am happy for you in my heart
But you are my one regret, it's true

I wish I could make you understand
My life is not the way I planned
I just have one regret, it's true
I cannot spend my life with you
Wish I could turn back the hands of time
Then move them forward and you'd be mine
Yes, one regret it's true
I wanted to spend forever with you

Yes one regret it's true
I wanted
To spend
Forever
With
You!

MEMORY PAGE

Mindslide

You know we can learn a lot from the forces of Nature
Storms brew up when temperatures are in disaccord
They intensify and build to dangerous proportions
Can cause irreparable damage, placing humans in positions they
can't even afford

Whoa!....We've got to watch out for the forces of Nature!

Tornadoes, Windstorms, Hurricanes and such!
The warm mixing with the cool causing patterns we can't touch,
Building fear in hearts because of forces we can't control,
Causing devastation, stripping lives of past memories,
Lives torn in half, no longer whole

Whoa!....We've got to watch out for the forces of Nature!

Like the forces of Nature are the Storms of Love,
Love is truly a natural element, an inborn desire of every
Soul
To be filled with it constitutes a quiet and solitude of the
mind
To be starved of it creates feelings of inadequacy, that
emotional feeling of
being half not whole.

Whoa! ...Watch out for the Storms of Love!

Mental anguish from pain of deceit and emotional neglect,
coupled with the words "I love you",
That's the cool mixed with the warm that causes Love
Storms,
Causes lack of respect
Causes gusts of such extreme proportions, causes the Red of
Love to turn Blue

Whoa!…Watch out for the Storms of Love!

And then here come the Mindslides….you ask what are
those?
You say you love me and expect me to flip,
To forget the pain and hurt, to forget the neglect
But it takes time to heal from the damaging affects of Love
Storms
See the Mindslides keep making me slip

Whoa!….Watch out for the Mindslides!

Believe me, there are times when a foundation becomes so
fragile
Nature has rocked it to the core
No patching up to the surface can remotely create what
existed before
So what currently stands needs to be condemned, maybe
rebuilt from ground up
Or maybe folks just realize it's time to clear it out, give up!

Whoa!…Watch out for unsteady foundations!

Is it worth living on this shaky ground?
When Mindslides are keeping you awake at night
When trust is so gone and you keep wondering why you are
around
When you feel like you are suffocating from the thick air
When you feel paralyzed, scared to move left or right
When you are realizing you no longer have the energy to
fight
Yes the Mindslides are overtaking you,
Sometimes staying may be life threatening…so don't be a
fool!

MEMORY PAGE

_____

_____

_____

_____

_____

_____

_____

_____

_____

_____

_____

_____

_____

_____

_____

_____

_____

Today Is The Day

Yes I'm a sistah of strength, just look me in the eyes,
You can't can you? Because my strength you despise!

It's killin' you 'cause I'm self-sufficient
Are you intimidated because I'm efficient?

It's no reflection on you brotha, no attack on your manhood!
A strong sistah is an asset, just wish you understood!

You see, I can pull you up, when you feel you're fallin' down
A weak sistah would just leave you alone to drown

Make up your mind brotha, today is the day!
Make up your mind brotha, should I go or stay?

If you turn your back on me brotha, you would be doin'
yourself an injustice!
Yes, I'm independent, so I can handle your business

And you know my love is unconditional because your
material things mean nothin' to me,
Unlike that weak sistah over there who only understands the
things she can see!

Yes I can cook, clean and take care of you brotha man,
But don't think my strength only limits me to that kind of
plan

Brotha, I can give you love, real lovin'
Give me a chance and stop buggin'

Let this sistah show you what a strong woman's lovin' is all
about

Trust me, you'll be beggin' and comin' back for more without
a doubt!

You got it brotha? Good lovin', lovin' from the soul
This sistahs ready, stop puttin' me on hold!

Get it together brotha, let me know is it a go?
Tell me now! This sistah's got to know!

I'm tellin' you right now, if you can't handle me brotha

This sistah's takin' this good lovin'
And findin' her another!

Yes, I'm strong, I admit it!

Aint nothin' wrong with that, just accept it!

Stop stringin' me along, this is it!

Today is the day, make up your mind or I'll split!

MEMORY PAGE

Damsel In Distress

Girls dream of that Prince in shining armor
You know the one on the White Horse
Just waited in my castle for him to appear
Looked out my window and let down my hair
He climbed up and rescued me...nope I wasn't pressed!
Never knew that after I hopped on the horse,
I could become a Damsel in Distress!

Sat in that castle for many a year
Just waiting for that moment in time
Envisioned my wedding day
It was crystal clear
But somewhere in the Storybook there was a missing line.

The Storybook says Cinderella lived happily ever after
I don't believe the story went that way
I bet right now that Prince has driven her crazy
He's probably fat and lazy
Bet she's tired of talking and wish he'd get a grip
Bet she's wishing that glass slipper never fit!

Wasn't Snow White the one that fell asleep?
Then with a kiss was awakened
Then off into the Sunset they rode, oh how sweet
Do you think they really told the truth?
No one probably reported she was married to a brut
Drinking and staying out all night,
Bet she's wishing she was back with those dwarfs living a
simple life.

Could Sleeping Beauty have had a fairer story?
Another Princess awakened from a trance
Rescued by another Man on a White horse,

Bet she's now explaining her story to a Jury,
How she ended up with a miserable plight,
How she had to for her life take flight,
Yep from the man who was supposed to protect her.
What an Irony, now the fairy tale is a blur!

Yes what an Irony!

That's what I say

How did my fairy tale end up this way!

Who would have ever guessed?

That after I hopped on his horse.....

I would become A Damsel in Distress?

MEMORY PAGE

Thru The Tears

Like dew dripping from the trees at early dawn
Were the tears I shed for you this morn
Cried myself to sleep last night
Woke up and still cryin' over our plight

With heavy heart I try to lift myself up
Reality settling in realizin' this battle will be tough
How will I go on without you?
You keep tellin' me I'm strong, that I'll make it thru

I'm not feelin' strength you say I possess
I can't envision future happiness
I'm gonna miss your calls, your smile, your touch
Can't savor the kisses that I love so much

You said the pain you are feelin' is just as intense
You said we knew when we started this could be the
consequence
Never meant to hurt you babe…was this a big mistake?
Thought I could handle this…but there's too much at stake

Thru the tears, from the depth of my soul
Know that your presence will be in my heart, you know you
make me whole
I'm bound in an arrangement with no quick fix
Couldn't focus on you and it, the two could not mix

Thru the tears, I wonder whether this decision I will regret
You told me to just release you…let you go…let you step
Why does this choice not feel good?
I feel violently shaken from the ground upon which we once
stood

Who knows what the future will hold for me
Don't you wonder in a few years where each of us will be?
Just know that thru the tears, strength will come
I pray that in future times our paths may cross and we may
still become one

"Mo" Love

LOVE IS BEAUTIFUL, WHEN IT'S RIGHT!

(Cherish special moments with your King or Queen)

MEMORY PAGE

First Love

Looking at her glowing face, her beaming eyes reveal
She's been hit with one of the most beautiful experiences of
life, one she can't conceal

Her face flush with the thrill, her heart skipping beats,
Her fingers and palms just damp with perspiration as her
body temperature heats

Boiling over with emotions as she turns around and catches
another glance,
It's her first love; she's filled with excitement, almost entering
a trance.

And the air seems so perfect, not too hot and not too cold,
Just fresh from his breath and his voice is as fine gold.

Overwhelmed now by his presence, can she keep this first
love feeling forever in her memories?
She knows she will, this memory cherish, it's as if it is
suspended in the passing breeze.

MEMORY PAGE

Oh Sweet Innocence

Swinging freely, no restraints!
Enjoying youth, Oh sweet innocence!
Don't steal my freedom; don't change this pace,
No aging for me, fancy free in life's race!
Not a care in the world, just enjoying life,
Little responsibility, little strife!
To be free to explore the world, no strings can anyone pull,
Paris, Rome, Italy, wow my life can be full!
To love, to love not, to look when I please!
To dance upon meadows, to float with the breeze!
So I'll flirt around you,
Middle age? No way!
I'm enjoying my sweet innocence; yes here is where I'll stay!

MEMORY PAGE

_____

_____

_____

_____

_____

_____

_____

_____

_____

_____

_____

_____

_____

_____

_____

_____

My Favorite Things

The warm glow of sunshine on my sun kissed face,
Grains of sand running through my toes,
Fresh, crisp, breeze whispering in my ears,
Moonlit evenings, twinkling stars

The giggling playfulness in little ones voices,
Warmth and coziness in Grandma's kitchen,
Comfort and calm from Mommy's arms,
Tender kiss and caress of the one I love

Tempting aroma of my morning Java,
Curling up in my favorite chair,
Take me away in a soothing bath,
Wine in crystal, soft candlelight,
Mellow tones play, as the fireplace crackles

Ah yes, these are a few of my favorite things!

MEMORY PAGE

Serenade Me

Gentle, delicate, soft, oh so sweet
Longing, living for your gentle caress
Desiring that only you embrace my soul
That my chills will melt away with your warmth

Will you save your serenade for me?
Anticipating your soothing melody
Your mellow tones to encircle me
Your base notes to run right through me

Yes save your serenade for me
I will cherish, hold it and protect it
For troubled times in my mind it will replay
For joyful times a reminder it will serve

Only you can send my heart a float
Only your voice can bring me serenity
Only you can play the strings of my soul
Please save your serenade for me

MEMORY PAGE

Memories Past

Remember my love the first time we met?
MEMORIES PAST, HOW QUICKLY WE FORGET

The glance we exchanged our hearts locked!
MEMORIES PAST, NOW OUR MINDS ARE BLOCKED

Close your eyes and just go back
MEMORIES PAST, CAN WE GET BACK ON TRACK?

I miss those days, those innocent days!
MEMORIES PAST, WHEN THE LOVE SONGS PLAYED

You would gently kiss me and stroke my hair
MEMORIES PAST, INTO MY EYES YOU WOULD STARE

We could talk for hours and hours
MEMORIES PAST, OH THE CARDS AND FLOWERS!

Somewhere along the line did we miss a link?
MEMORIES PAST, SIT BACK, REFLECT, THINK

Can we repair the damaged cords, make amends?
MEMORIES PAST, TOO MUCH SHARED TO LET IT END

My dear, so happy am I for the good times to reflect upon
MEMORIES PAST, LET'S VOW TOGETHER TO MOVE ON!

MEMORY PAGE

The Maze

You and I are in the center standing back to back,
Surrounded by a maze, called life, deciding on a track

It's such a hard decision when you are in the center looking
out,
Don't know where to begin, can't figure out should you cry,
laugh or shout

Although neither of us is fancy free,
I'm dying inside to meet the one who is traveling this maze
with me.

Remember it was your gesture, your gentle voice, inviting
eyes that drew me in,
I must admit, I cherish the thought of meeting you once
again!

I've tiptoed and chosen a path outside my comfort zone,
I'm moving along into territory for me that is quite
unknown.

Tell me what you are feeling, what's in your heart,
What is your life's story and where would you like me to
play a part?

You are right about this maze; we will have to see how we
make it thru,
And no matter what path we choose, it's gonna be fun
working it out with you!

MEMORY PAGE

_____

_____

_____

_____

_____

_____

_____

_____

_____

_____

_____

_____

_____

_____

_____

_____

_____

_____

_____

Caramelized

Like Caramel I melt when I come near your heat
When I look into your eyes my heart just skips beats
Can't explain how you've turned my world upside down
Got me spinnin' in circles 'round and 'round

Yep Caramelized!

No better word to describe
How since we've met I've been on this incredible ride
Like warm Caramel that slides down ice-cream
My body craves yours even in my dreams

Yep Caramelized!

What a position to be in
It kills me when I don't know where you've been
You monopolize my thoughts baby, day and night
It's a struggle just to have you out of my sight

Yep Caramelized!

Your skin is like caramel, Baby
It's sun kissed!

Your kisses warm and ignite me
Your touch just caramelizes me

So don't be afraid to touch me!

Yep I'm Caramelized!

MEMORY PAGE

Feelin' The Rhythm

I'm feelin' the rhythm of your heartbeat
I'm feelin' you throb as our bodies meet
I'm feelin' the rhythm as I wrap around you
I'm feelin' the rhythm, are you feelin' it too?

The drumbeats begin as I enter your space
And as I approach you, they pick up the pace
As my eyes meet yours the stronger the beat
Then a thunderous roll when I feel your body heat

Do you hear the cymbals? A delicate ring
That increases intensity, for you and I they sing
Special notes, sweet melody, smooth and steady
Your body language says, for me you are ready

An orchestra of strings, horns and percussion
We created our own rhythm and precision
We harmonized, we blended our tune
We've reached a crescendo as high as the moon

Could you ever have imagined?

We could create such a masterpiece as that?

Such harmony, baby!

I felt your heartbeat

I felt you throb

Yes....I felt the rhythm!

MEMORY PAGE

Traveling the Serengeti

Loving you is like traveling the Serengeti
Wild yet mystical, serene yet sensual

Have you ever been? To the Serengeti…that is?

The plains take you as far as your eyes can see
That's how far your love takes me

The desert there is parched, golden from the sun
Your love for me is golden and that's why I know you are the
one

Hush, listen to the solitude, it's the quiet before the storm
Your love starts so serene and then you get warm

Feel the thunderous roar as the wildlife engulfs the Serengeti
Your love is wild and thunderous as you overtake me

Observe the Hugh of light as the sun sets over that African
land, like a mirage out of a dream
And so it is as you settle upon me, your Nubian Queen

Tonight we traveled across the Serengeti

Yes….you took me across the Wild Serengeti!

MEMORY PAGE

One Fall Day

It was one fall day I will never forget
The air was so crisp, the day was perfect
We allowed our worries to fly away with the breeze
We shared past regrets as the wind blew through the trees
Then we dreamed and we planned of future times we would
spend
Would the day just stand still....would the time just extend?

Seemed like Nature just smiled upon the two of us that day
Seemed the sun shined down and gave us it's rays
Seemed the sky was a blue made especially for us
Seemed the leaves danced along with the light wind gusts

Did you see how the water flowed so peacefully?
Did hear how the birds sang so blissfully?
Did you smell the scent nature sprayed in the air?
Did you feel the emotions of joy she wanted us to share?

Your kisses were gentle on the beautiful fall day
Your embrace warmed me up took my chills right away
Your soulful expressions captured me from the start
Your respectful position is what captivates my heart

Yes the perfect fall day
The perfect spot
The perfect companion
The perfect setting

There is absolutely nothing I would change about that day
Thanks for the moment in time you have placed in my
memory
Tenderly placed
To be cherished
Time spent with you
One fall day

MEMORY PAGE

Wish I Could Have Been Your Sunshine

You said you had some stormy days
You said life cast some clouds over you
You said you learned life's lessons now changed some ways
Baby it's o.k. with me it's happened to me too

But I wish I could have been your sunshine then
Wish I could have dried up those rainy days
Wish I could have held you tight through those times
Wish I could have warmed you with my rays
Wish I could have
Just wish I could have

You said you had pains and perils
You said you are glad you are now on the other side
You said life looks good, you've grown and that's good
Baby I don't judge you...I admire your new strides

I know I can't fix the past
But know that I am here for you now!
Know that when you feel overcast
When those clouds settle in
When the downpours begin
Baby I will be here for you any time of the year
Let me shine on you, Baby
Let me warm you all over
Let me be your sunshine

Wish I could

Wish I could

Wish I could

MEMORY PAGE

Sumthin bout you

You asked me what was I feelin' bout you
When I'm 'round you
When I'm in your space

Couldn't find words at the time to verbally express
I just know it's sumthin' bout you!

I told you the rays you emit just warm me
When I lean on you...hmm, hmm, hmm
I love when you just look at my face

I love your aura, baby
I love your touch
It's sumthin' bout you
That I love so much

It's your laid back style
It's your strut
It's your no nonsense talk
It's your bee, bop, bop!
It's your piercing eyes...I love that nose
Hmm, hmm, hmm...and those lips!

For real, it's your soul
It's all the stuff that makes you whole
It's your talent and your inner being
It's sumthin' bout you!

I want you to know I mean no disrespect
Don't know how ya feel
Don't know where ya are
Don't know where ya stand

I've just had time to reflect
Yep! There's sumthin' bout you!

I wanted you to know
There's sumthin' bout you!

Hmm, hmm, hmm...

Sumthin bout you!

MEMORY PAGE

_____

_____

_____

_____

_____

_____

_____

_____

_____

_____

_____

_____

_____

_____

_____

_____

_____

The Pleasure's All Mine

From the moment I met you our souls engaged
I knew in my heart, this would be no passing stage
The vibes you released, honey, encircled me
I knew where we are today was meant to be

That first touch was electrifying
No words can I express, just no denying
Baby, you locked me in, with your inviting smile
I was ready from then, wanted you to put me on trial

And when our lips met it was all over then
Didn't want to rush you babe, but I wanted to know when
When would you let me love you, satisfy your every need
Yeah, run your cup over, baby, I was ready to plead

So here we are in the heat of it all
Got a rush from your voice when you finally called
Babe, the pleasure's all mine, tonight is your night
No more words, just relax and enjoy this flight

This evening's so special to me
I've been dreaming about it for a long time, you see
Could picture this moment in time
Satisfying you, the pleasure's all mine

MEMORY PAGE

Passion

Passion to me is that inner driving force
It's that feeling deep in my intestines, driving me towards
this course
It's a desire so deep, that words can't even explain
All I know is when I'm near you the passion is all there, you
ignite my flame!

What is your passion, baby?
'Cause my passion is to be with you!
What is your passion baby?
Is your passion to be with me too?

When we were together that flame we ignited started to
grow
Our bodies felt the passion, juices started to flow
We stopped short, we let that fire flicker out,
Was it timing? What made us stop? What was that all about?

Your touch sent chills straight down my spine
Your kisses your caress, I still can't get them out of my mind
That's why I know, baby, you did something to me that day
Been wantin' to tell you for a while, but couldn't find the
right words to say!

When I'm singin' the blues, baby
I can't help but think of you
I just have to smile, baby, at the things you say and do
See passion is strong
I can hold out as long
As I know you feel the passion too!

Just let me know are you feeling it too?
Are you feeling it?

PASSION!
Are you feeling it?
PASSION!

Passion makes you breathless
Passion makes you fearless
How else could I have mustered up the strength to let you
know
'Cause my passion is to be with you!

MEMORY PAGE

_____

_____

_____

_____

_____

_____

_____

_____

_____

_____

_____

_____

_____

_____

_____

_____

_____

_____

Keeps Comin' Back To You

No matter how hard I try
To run away from what we have here
No matter how hard I try
My heart keeps comin' back to you, dear
Wrong or right?...I'm torn in two
Soul searching keeps me comin' back to you

Magnetism....I've been drawn into your magnetic field!
Your electric energy surrounds me like a protective shield
I've tried to break the circuit....but I can't shut it down
Babe your pull is intense...it keeps me comin' around

Stimulation....The tingling I get from your voice, your touch
Hmm, Hmm, Hmm baby...It's the things you say that make
me blush
The way you smile...the way you laugh
The way you make me feel special....and that's only the half
Of the things you do
That keep me comin' back to you

Progression.....Yes movement forward we have agreed upon
Formed a union of sorts which makes us one
A meeting of the minds in a special way
Blending of mind & soul day by day
No one else may understand the why & how...but we know
why we do what we do
And it's that reason that keeps me comin' back to you!

Magnetism, Stimulation, Progression

Yes strong & powerful expressions

They are so us

Keep pulling me in… Keep me in your magnetic field

Keep energizing me…stimulating me

With your smile

With your touch

Let's move forward baby

Progress is good

A meeting of the mind

You are deep baby

You are soooo deep

Magnetism

Stimulation

Progression

Keeps me comin' back to you!

MEMORY PAGE

Must Be Everlasting

Together we have climbed some of the highest mountains
We've weathered the roughest of seas
Wrestled with some great Giants
And look around babe it's still just you and me

We've had some times we second guessed this union
Looked at each other with disgust
Said some things we regretted later
Had some episodes of mistrust
But look at us now, we are survivors

They say heartache brings you closer
They say the rough times tighten the bond
They say sweet times are coming
They say as we go through changes we grow more fond
And they are right!...bring on the sugar, yes the sugar, baby!

This love must be everlasting
Can't imagine an obstacle we can't take on
Don't even want to imagine, life without you
You're stuck with me, honey
Ain't a thing can break this bond

Elmers ain't got nothin' on us baby!

We're stronger than cement glue!
Bring it on!
We can handle it!
This bond is strong!
And
it's gettin' sweet
like sugar cane

like honey
sweet!
And best of all
yeah…..EVERLASTING!

MEMORY PAGE

_____

_____

_____

_____

_____

_____

_____

_____

_____

_____

_____

_____

_____

_____

_____

_____

_____

_____

_____

_____

Soulwife

Man, I can't explain to you how deep we be
Ain't no words to express what ya mean to me

When you look at me your eyes pierce thru to my soul
The value of times we spend are worth more to me than gold

Man, no money, no material things could ever measure up to
what we've got
This bond is intense, it's so deep, 'cause it's cool...but then it's
HOT!

Never quite understood the true feelin' of havin' a
SOULMATE
But I feel it now, 'cause you and I are livin' in that state

It's so much more than a physical thing
It's mind wrapped up with soul, it's feelings that make ya
wanna sing!

It's knowin' ya got a buddy for life
It's the arms ya know ya can run to for comfort, when ya
feelin' strife

It's you Man, you're the one
Amazin' what we've created together, can't undo it, 'cause it's
done!

Soulmates baby, wrapped tight, you've got my back and I've
got yours
Only God can see what the future has in store!

But this, Man, I know for sure

Our connection is so beautiful because our intentions are
pure

Yeah, right now ain't no license or ring
But that don't mean a thing!

Make no doubt about it our love is for life!
So Baby, right now, think of me as your SOULWIFE!

"Mo" tivation

FROM PAIN AND LOVE WE GAIN STRENGTH AND
DETERMINATION!

**(Get back up on that horse, rebuild your
Castle and ride off into the sunset, for real!)**

MEMORY PAGE

From Birth to Death

Expelled from water, warmth & security
Into a world cold, unknown & far from purity
Scared, crying out to be enveloped,
Comfort found in the arms of the one who my character will
help develop

Happy, bouncing enjoying the bright days of youth
No troubles, worries or cares, life feels full of simple truth
A circle of family & love to be engulfed in
Protected from all that's evil, guarded from sin

Tumultuous times those teenage years!
Unpredictable emotions, unspoken fears
In love, young desires, now side by side with a mate
Now beginning this cycle anew waiting on a due date

Rocking gently, nodding frequently even forgetting at times,
Family grown, gone, loneliness sets in as the clock chimes
Time has ticked from the time of birth, where has it gone?
Peace, solitude, rest now, I've moved on.

MEMORY PAGE

Her Eyes Reveal It All

Look into her eyes, deep into her soul
Her eyes reveal it all, a story to be told
A picture of outward beauty, epitome of grace

Her eyes reveal pain that can never be erased
Brought into this world by a mother so young
Abandoned to die, yet her life was not done
A fighter from the start she proved to be

Passed from home to home lived in poverty
Married as a solvent for her miserable years
Was beaten, mistreated, her eyes reveal tears
No longer would she accept mediocrity
Worth so much more, time for the world to see

Put the refuse in her life where it belongs
Deep in the dungeon, now she is strong
Her eyes reveal peace, her story she shares
To enrich lives and alleviate fears

Mature woman now, her eyes reveal at last
Success despite an unfortunate past
She glides with grace, holds her head high
Can't no one stop you, so reach for the sky!

MEMORY PAGE

I Shall Be Victorious!

Oh, wretched pain that aches my heart,
I feel you as deep as my belly!
Wrapping my inner organs tearing me apart,
Why can't I just throw you asunder?
Yes, can I cast you away never to return?
Promise me in the forest of my past you will stay,
Never more to encroach upon my thoughts,
To lay respite forever more!
Aye! May I be granted peace and serenity!
Bring true love within my reach!
Less the sorrow, aches and pains,
Less the pangs, pressures and perils,
Pull me up from this dungeon,
From this maze of seeming doom
Wretched pain, thy overcast shadow shall be removed!
A new day shall dawn!
I shall overcome you!
I shall feel Victory!

MEMORY PAGE

Never Abandon Hope

There lies a desire for love that can be despair,
It creeps up at times, leaves me gasping for air.

They say the heart is treacherous and desperate,
And with this welled up feeling within I believe it.

Feelings trapped so deep down they can't escape,
Should I abandon all hope of true love, my heart would truly
break.

I'm in the midst of a love jungle, vines twisted up in knots,
Emotions swinging to and fro, tell me, will this ever stop?

Depression from the anxieties, lows so deep I can't explain,
Rivers, oceans & seas deep are the hurt, the anger, and the
pain.

And then the highs that come when he found me,
He pulled me up from depths so deep,
Praised me, loved me, held me, lifted me so high I will no
longer creep.

Gone are the days of pain, sorrow, hurt, anger and despair,
You have entered into my life and joy and happiness we will
forever share.
A lesson so valuable I have learned, by having you save me
from my downward slope,
When you need love to help you through tumultuous times,
never abandon hope!

MEMORY PAGE

The Inner Me

I'm at a point in my life that has never hit me before,
It's that time that I must decide who am I living for

Is it for husband, kids, friends, or for the world?
I've decided the answers come from a special little girl

Big dreams she had that got lost in the shuffle
She grew older, lost touch with her dreams & life hit her with
hustle & bustle

Realizing now those little girl aspirations & desires have
really never gone away
They lied dormant, now awakened & are here to stay!

That little girl is now ready to live for her, you see
Soul-searched & found that little girl is the Inner Me

So I'm moving ahead now with vision and a new attitude
No longer living without purpose, no time to sit & brood

I love the Inner Me, I'm at peace now with my life,
I'm a happier Mother, Friend, Family Member and Wife

I know now what I want, what I deserve and will accept
Now, not all can handle the new attitude I project

But the Inner Me realizes it's o.k. & helps me move on
What matters is, I'm happy & I know where I belong!

MEMORY PAGE

Calm the Sea

My life has flashed before my eyes
Like a boat on waters beneath blue skies
Bright sunny day, crystal clear expanse
Sounds of Sea Gulls, the beauty they enhance

Drifting smoothly with no turmoil in sight
Upon peaceful waters both day & night
Feet dangling aboard into the soothing sea
Solitude exists, just my thoughts & me

Suddenly a change, swift, without warning!
Massive waves begin to form, there's storming
Tearing & lashing against my boat
Frightened, can I stay afloat?

Have mercy on me oh great expanse of sea
I'm a fragile, lonely soul, can't you see?
Spare me anymore wrath, you've weakened me!
Return my boat, please calm the sea!

MEMORY PAGE

Expansion

Expand your mind
Take it to the highest level
Stop hindering your growth
Realize your potential

Realize your worth
Let no one undermine you
Let no one demean you
Let no one cramp your belief in your abilities

Oh they will try, there is no doubt
But you have the ability to stamp their negativity out
Show them it is simply their own insecurities that cause
them to feel the need to undermine you
It is their own cowardliness that causes them to only focus
on your flaws
When you know that you are beautiful, talented and capable

With words you need not always retaliate, though
With actions, the strength you possess will show
Dream big dreams
Dream Grandiose!
Know that you are worth it all
Know that no one and nothing but you can hold back success

So throw away the reigns that hold you back
Cut off the strings that tie you down
Open wide the cage doors you reside within

Take flight!
Expand your mind!
Take it to the highest level!

111

MEMORY PAGE

_____

_____

_____

_____

_____

_____

_____

_____

_____

_____

_____

_____

_____

_____

_____

_____

_____

_____

_____

Black Man Show Me Your Strength

Black Man
Don't tell me how strong you are

SHOW ME!

Show me the power of your walk
By the strides you make to leave a positive mark on society

Flex your muscles
So I can see how you use your arms
And empower your brothers to action

Show me that with your eyes of insight
You have the ability to look into a matter and
Take decisive action

Don't tell me how strong you are

SHOW ME!
Show me that with a tongue of intelligence
You speak words of wisdom and not foolishness

Impress me with your progressive mentality

Show me that embodied within that head of yours
Is a mind full of purpose and passion

Show me that you cherish your God given responsibility
To care for those who are your own

Black man it is not your ebony skin and your physique
that move me
It is the STRENGTH you show me

SO SHOW ME!

MEMORY PAGE

Falling Down

I'm Falling Down
Spiraling into an abyss of darkness
This day is taking me down into oblivion
Too much to handle

Too much stress
I'm feelin' like there's no way out of this mess
My skies are turning gray 'cause I'm worn down
Floods of emotions have caused my smile to turn into a
frown

I know I must rise
At least that's what my intellect says

But my heart is weighed down and
The head and the heart aren't connecting today
So down I fall

With a see-saw of emotions I try to contend
Up and Down
Strong then Weak
Laugh then Cry
Faith then Fear

God, when will it end?

Trying to take this thing hour by hour
Because beyond that I've lost the power
To have control
Those dark clouds have formed and blocked my vision

And since my sight is obstructed my eyes and my feet

Can no longer connect today
To create a straight path and so I miss my step

And I keep Falling Down
But reality for me will never be
I'm falling and I can't get up

No, that's not me
You see

I was created with the intellectual capacity
To clearly see
That to rise defies gravity

Nature makes it easy for us to stay down
So I guess I have decided to become unnatural
To create my own laws

Because when I decide to remove the clouds that have
blocked my vision
And my eyes and my feet reconnect
I will lift up!

I will remove the weights from around my heart
And cast them into the sea!

And when I chose to climb off that see-saw of emotions
You will look at me
And you will see a beautiful thing

That like a bird with clipped wing
I healed
Spread my wings
And chose to be free!

MEMORY PAGE

I Define Me

I am a beautiful black woman
Living in a society that wishes to mold me
But my self-respect won't allow anyone but myself
To define me

I don't have a need to be trendy
Insubstantial judgments rarely do offend me
I am who I am
I choose freely who I wish to be
It is not hard to fathom
How I define me

I don't need to speak in Ebonics
Pretending to be hooked on phonics
Just to get where I fit in
With shallow cliques and deceitful friends
God made me beautifully articulate, you see
And I define me

I don't need a man standing by my side
To attain a sense of self-pride
A strong man's love is a commodity to be known
But before a man undermines my strengths
I'd gladly stand alone

Do I possess weaknesses?
Yes, that's for sure
But what makes me the queen I am
Is my ability to endure

You see, I define me
Though it's not always done easily

Because the perils of a weak society
Often catch us in an unjust propriety

They say an educated woman is something to be feared
But as she chooses her path and defines who she is
She is something to be revered

I was not presented with a silver spoon at the time of my
birth
But I didn't wait around for the world to determine my
intrinsic worth

I chose to stand out
Never waiting for a hand out
I chose never to wait on destiny
When I was perfectly capable of defining me

Intrigued by my intrepidity
Some ridicule the woman I am
Sometimes my own sisters and brothers
Hey I have the master plan

You see, I define me
Please take off your blinders and see

This world won't give credit where it's due
Until you stand on your own
and decide to define you!

Original Author Unknown

(Adjustments have been made to original text by Monique Stubbs-Hall)

MEMORY PAGE

_____

_____

_____

_____

_____

_____

_____

_____

_____

_____

_____

_____

_____

_____

_____

_____

_____

I Will Not Settle!

"Settle for less" is not the best slogan for me!

I have more in store than you could ever see.

Abundant in my thoughts, prospective broad and wide,

Shaking off the mundane, insignificant and frivolous from my side

Building an Aura of Strength, Karma of Purpose, Stature of Belief

Exploding mind boggles and jagged edges to give relief!

Non stop, moving with haste towards the goal,

On an Orient Express of minds, locomotive patterns with no hold

Enormity of growth unheard & unseen

Possibilities unfolding endlessly towards the dream!

No there is no time to Settle for Less!

MEMORY PAGE

The Flow

You can't possibly understand
what I possess in my hand

You obviously don't have a clue,
what my mind orchestrates me to do

The combination of my pen & my mind, like deep rivers
produce a flow
Unless you too have acquired it you just wouldn't know

The richness of my ink as it flows over a page
Running deep feelings, expressions of love entwined with
rage

Can't no one fault me when I write, see that's the beauty of
the flow
My energy is released; my spirit soars, out comes my inner
soul

Man, when you asked me to stop what I love so much
When you forbid me to express my flow, my special touch

I knew right then you didn't have a clue
Of the depth of what you were asking me to do

I know you take what I write so personally
that you miss conceptually,
what I see
and who I be

Yes you are correct when you say,
"Poetry is deep it comes from the heart"

But brotha you don't understand how things flow once I start

Once I place ink to paper, like floodgates opening up, is my
flow
I can't stop
won't stop
I've got to write
I've got to speak it ,
so the world will know
And to suppress my talent
damn it up
let the ink dry
and leave it be?

What are you asking me to agree upon
evidently you just can't see

Take yourself out of the middle and just let yourself grow
Realize poetry is simply an exchange of life's journeys,
release your own insecurities,
relax and enjoy my flow!

MEMORY PAGE

Mommy

It was in your womb I was conceived
Expelled from you, so I could breathe
In your arms found comfort and rest
Laid peacefully upon your breast

It was you who nurtured me and wiped my tears
Yes your sweet voice that calmed my fears
Sacrificed your dreams to stay home
Picked me up from school so I was not alone

Never once complaining about your lot in life
Cherish child and husband, wow an awesome wife
Trained and groomed me into the lady I've become
Grace and charm, I know where they come from

Mommy, can you believe I'm raising children of my own?
I'm married and facing life's challenges, oh my how I've
grown
Warm memories of my youthful years, keeps me moving on
Yes, this ode is to you, this is your song

MEMORY PAGE

_____

_____

_____

_____

_____

_____

_____

_____

_____

_____

_____

_____

_____

_____

_____

_____

_____

_____

Daddy

Your #1 I am, in so many ways
Firstborn I am, the joy of your days
Your #1 fan, more than you will ever know
Always my Daddy, guiding my growth

My stronghold, my pillar of support
No matter what, you were my forte
Looking back, I'm so glad you were there
Your wisdom I cherish, it's molded my years

Womanless without Daddy by my side
Reassuring me as I took life's ride
Teaching me what from others is expected
Arms wide open, when at times I felt rejected

Time from your schedule you allotted for me
Cherished those times as I sat on your knee
Daddy, my hero, the wind beneath my wings
Daddy this ode is to you, I will always your praises sing

Acknowledgements

No large undertaking can come to fruition without a network of team players. Although I had a vision and a dream to accomplish this project, there are so many who infused their belief in my abilities into me and helped me turn this dream into reality!

Special thanks to my husband, Charles, for his belief, encouragement and support. To my three little inspirations, my children (Gordon, Monet and Chloe) who have stood by my side and whose hugs and kisses have helped me ride many a wave, through this period of healing. I acknowledge my sister Cristal for her unconditional love and support. To my Mary Kay Cosmetic family, who continue to be such a positive circle of influence in my life. Uncle Allan and Aunt Helena, words cannot express my appreciation for your continued support of my efforts. Eternal thanks to my parents, Christopher and Stephanie Stubbs for instilling in me a strong work ethic and a survival instinct beyond belief!

Tracey Winder-Davis, thank you for motivating me to share my work for the benefit of others who are experiencing blues and need healing too. Jearlean Taylor, there are no words to describe the inspiration I receive just from being in your presence! William Sledge, thanks for your continued efforts to promote my talent! Robert Stephens your photography has added the perfect touch to the completion of this piece, thank you.

My Sincere Thanks to Each and Every Reader

Love "Mo"

About the Author

Elegance, grace, coupled with a sense of humour, yes that's "Mo" (Monique Stubbs-Hall). She has a Million Dollar smile, that will light up any room, but a Million Dollar attitude to accompany it. Don't allow, though, the exterior to fool you into believing that "Mo" is naïve and untouched from the perils of life.

A native of Nassau, Bahamas, "Mo" was brought up in a very spiritual household with strict but loving parents who she accredits for her bubbly, positive, outgoing personality coupled with a strong work ethic. Having traveled abroad with her family and gaining exposure to a variety of ethnic backgrounds, she has no problem transcending her inspirational words to any type of audience, she just loves people! Growing up in a sheltered environment, "Mo" was totally unprepared to discover that her beautiful marriage of 13 years was nothing more than a façade. "Mo" had to come to grips with devastating discoveries that resulted in her making some life changing decisions. In order to avoid a complete emotional breakdown, she went through two years of medication treatment for depression and anxiety. It was through this period that she realized she had two choices, to wallow in self pity and become immobilized or to pick herself up and choose to enjoy life. Of course, no one could ever imagine the emotional devastation and pain that comes from deception unless they have experienced it.

When "Mo" stopped being mad, she decided to turn her energies into healing by focusing on being strong and for the sake of her three inspirations (Gordon, Monet and Chloe). When she looks into their eyes every day she is reminded of why she must continue to set an example for them, so that they will acquire what she calls BBA (Bounce Back Ability) as they experience life's roller coasters. She humbly realizes her own imperfections and has used lessons learned from trials and errors, lots of prayers, along with pouring herself into writing, as the best methods of healing.

Despite her painful experience she is still a strong believer in the institution of marriage, "because it's beautiful, when it's right". She is now remarried to her supportive husband, Charles, who she is looking forward to spending eternity with!

ISBN 141208796-1